When Felons Cry

Melanie Mason James Hicks, Jr. Susanne Bunton Keya Jest

When Felons Cry

Publisher: KeyCity Publishing

Book Cover Designer: It Takes Faith Media

ISBN 9781736431467

Dedication

To my six grown Heartbeats: Javon, Rodney, Jasmine, Antwon, Aadiya & William. We have been through many storms, trials, and tribulations. But we stood together as a family. May this book be an encouragement to never give up on your dreams. The struggle is now over.

My Lifelines:
Pastor Kenny Grant, Pastor Valarie Jenkins Grimes, Pastor Jeffery Cummings, Hadiya Gumbs Rouse

My Heart 2 Heart Sisters Georgette & Susan, there are just no words of how I feel about you. You have gone far beyond the word sister. Thank you.

Keisha Lapsley, you met me at a time when I was truly broken. Thank you for not judging. Your support means more to me than you will ever know.

Thank You, Abba Father, for giving me a second chance. I will forever praise Your Name.

"Give your past mistakes to God, so He can turn them into miracles. "
– Author Unknown

Foreword

Foreword By: Pastor Kenny Grant

Tears have meaning. Only God knows the meaning of each tear that falls unbidden from crying eyes; however, be assured He DOES know and understands from whence they come. In the Bible, we see God took note of the tears of His people. Some of them were tears of grief and mourning, while some were from guilt and shame, but most tears' common root is pain. Yes, some tears flow from a sense of gladness, but I dare say that only the Lord knows how many more have fallen because of pain. The pain of abuse, abandonment, betrayal, loneliness, regret, and the likes. Scars prove an earlier wound, and wounds give evidence of pain that often expresses itself in tears.

Like most other things, Tears have their place and purpose in life, and it is God alone who can take the tears of pain and turn them into telescopes through which He might cause us to see worlds beyond the pain which brought the tears.

For those who come to faith in Christ, we can rest assured that He who holds us in His grip can turn our mess-ups into messages of His grace. We might also be assured that the One who also wept in pain over a lost city, at the grave of a dear friend and all alone in the garden, knows your pain and gives you the promise that "He will swallow up death in victory, and the Lord God will wipe away tears from all faces, and the rebuke of His people shall He take away from off all the earth; for the Lord hath spoken it." Is. 25:8

This volume will allow you to hear the cry and see the tears of some whose hurts, habits, and hang-ups have caused pain and tears for themselves as well as those they love. Their stories could very easily have been our own, but for the grace of God. The lessons they have learned and share with us because of God's grace are for our encouragement and profit. Learn the lessons that God has for you WHEN FELONS CRY.

Table of Contents

Melanie Mason

Introduction

Criminal, convict, delinquent, offender, con, jailbird, ex-con are a few synonyms that refer to those who have committed crimes. How many times have you heard or used those words? How often have you said he or she is a felon and change is not possible? How many times have you turned your back on someone that only wanted a second chance?

These words are labels and a reminder of the mistakes that were made. For some, these words will be forever embedded in their minds. Even though they paid the price for the crimes committed, there is a mindset still in a state of incarceration. It's hard to move forward when you are constantly reminded of your past. Those reminders are as simple as being denied housing or employment due to the criminal background. Not everyone is willing to give a second chance.

I have six children, four of which are young men. Each one has been subjected to the justice system. Each one has turned or is in the stages of turning themselves around. They did things I believe they truly regretted. Sometimes it took being arrested several times to encounter a new mindset. I always encouraged them to accept responsibility for their actions. Even though they know God is a God of second chances, it was somewhat difficult to experience the "second chance." I had to become the pusher, the intercessory, the encourager.

They will not be a statistic!

As I write this introduction, I too am reminded of a crime I committed in 2010, a justice-involved person. Yes, so many doors were closed due to the term that Georgia State gave me…FELON. To succeed and get out of the trap of bondage, I had to push, intercede and encourage myself. But I also had a strong relationship with several sisters and brothers who prayed and encouraged me. They became my lifelines. Most importantly, they did not judge or turn their backs on me.

I will not be a statistic! I am not a statistic!

As you read the testimonials in this powerful book, I urge you to reflect on your past. Think about the goodness of God and how His mercy, grace, and favor changed you because, yes, it could have been you. You may have a family member that is currently incarcerated. You may have a close friend that is a returning resident. What second chance can you give them? How can you get involved with nonprofit organizations to help change a Juvenile Impacted teen? How can you use your voice?

We all have a story. We all have a past. Four authors have come together to share their past, present, and future of hope. We each have our own individual experiences. We each have a unique voice. We each have the desire to impact and change the lives of others that are where we once were.

Our testimonies are open, honest, and transparent. Walk with us as we invite you into our lives, the good, the bad, the ugly, and the most vulnerable parts of our lives.

Again, some do not believe in second chances; this book is not for you. This book is for those who have walked in the redemption of knowing that God will provide a second, third, fourth, and as many chances needed to get it right to change lives and for Him to get the glory.

Melanie Mason is the CEO of Rise Up 2 Build Up, a ministry that connects communities with social or economic concerns. She is an advocate for those, whether male or female that have been or are currently involved with domestic violence, homelessness, single parenting, and those with derogatory backgrounds. She has a passion for assisting the broken, the battered, and the bruised by facilitating workshops, conferences, and speaking engagements. Her mission is that everyone she meets will not only RISE but also re-BUILD their lives so God may get the glory.

Arrested in 2010 and placed on an 8-year probation period, Melanie works to ensure that not only herself but also those formerly or currently incarcerated will not become a statistic. Her experience allows her to empathize with those fighting to turn their lives around.

In May of 2017, Melanie's first project, 'Releasing Your Pain For His Glory,' was completed with the assistance of her producer. It's a documentary dedicated to the families and individuals whose lives were affected by acts of domestic violence. In 2020 she co-authored "Lifting The Mask," a book of testimonies about women taking off their masks by becoming their authentic selves.

Melanie learned the importance of being an effective leader. She serves as a Team Launch Leader and Hospitality Leader with Radiant Church, Savannah, Ga. She is also a Certified Life Coach. When she is not working as a caterer, she visits different motels, serving those less fortunate. She provides toiletry items, food, and, more importantly, sharing the love of Christ. She is a Change Agent making a difference in the lives she touches.

Melanie Mason from Gastonia, NC, is a 1990 South Point High School graduate. She currently resides in Savannah, GA. She is the mother of six children and grandmother to three beautiful granddaughters. She served as the secretary at Christ's Community Church and as a former Board Member for Family Promise of Savannah. She currently serves as a Board Member for Divine Rest, Inc. Lastly, Melanie represents her Brand and Motto: Reaching 1 Person, 1 Family, 1 Day At A Time.

If you need a motivational speaker, life coach, facilitator, talk show host, panel, or conference host, please email me at riseup2buildup@gmail.com, or you may call me at 912.396.1668.

✠ Through The Storms ✠

"Pull down your pants, bend over, and cough," scary words to hear from someone that is two times bigger than you. Besides, these are not the words any female should want to hear, nor are they words that should be commanded and followed. Needless to say, these are the words that opened my eyes to the fact I was really being arrested, and what's more, I was not dreaming. It was a nightmare. October 12, 2010, was the day that changed my life forever. On this day, the State of Georgia gave me a name I never thought I would have, be known for, or even answer to FELON. How did I get to this point? Truth be told, to this day, I am still asking myself that very same question.

There is a saying, "we all have our demons." Anger was mine, and I did not know how to control it. I could go for months, a year without an episode. But when it came, I was a totally different person. Whomever or whatever was standing in my way when the explosion occurred would surely reap my wrath of hostility. Fury was an understatement. To be honest, I didn't know I had a problem with anger until after I started having children of my own. I hit my son so hard that he fell off the kitchen counter onto the floor on one occasion. When I picked him up, his little nose was bleeding. Thinking back to that day, I wish I had done more to help myself.

I was adopted. Not counting my stepbrother, who was way older than me; I was the only child for about twelve years. My adoptive mother was abusive. I remember the beatings and the cussing. I never heard the words "I love you"; therefore, I never learned how to love myself or someone else. I was noticeably quiet and pretty much kept to myself. I loved to read, and oh, how I loved school. School was my sanctuary, a safe haven. It was a place for me to go to get away from the 'noise' of a home that should have nurtured me. I could be sick as a dog, with a fever of 150, and I would still go to school. I would cry on snowy days and when school was out during the summer. School is where I wanted to be. It is where I needed to be. It is where I had to be.

Even though I desired to be at school morning, noon, and night, it still did not take the place of the hurt and pain I experienced when I was at home. One memory that will always be etched in my mind is when what started out as a normal school day ended with being beaten with a steel baseball bat. "You better not miss the bus!!" words that were screamed at me as I ran out the door with swollen legs and arms. Running to catch the bus. Running to my haven. I don't know what was worse, the pain from the bat or the embarrassment as the neighborhood kids looked at me laughing while I was getting on the bus. Whew! That was the longest bus ride. It seemed to have taken three hours to get to school that day. The whispers, the snickering. I only wanted someone to hold me and wipe the tears away…someone, anyone.

A few months later, I graduated from high school. A few weeks after graduation, Atlanta Job Corps was my way of escape. I left home and never looked back. The only regret I have was leaving my two adopted sisters behind. I will never forget standing outside of the Greyhound Station, hugging my two sisters with tears rolling down their faces, begging me to take them with me. Due to their age, they stayed behind and, unfortunately, continued to take on the wrath of our mother's anger. The same anger that unknowingly dwindled down onto me.

Atlanta, Georgia, a new beginning…but was it?

Out of all the places for a young, naïve girl to escape, Atlanta, Georgia, was not the place to go. I didn't know who I was. I didn't know how to take care of myself, to think for myself. I didn't know anything about life as a whole. I was the "go along to get along" type of girl. Always trying to please everyone and didn't like confrontation. I was easily persuaded by men, a trait that started as a teenager and followed me into adulthood.

My naiveness led me to have my first child at nineteen. I barely graduated from Job Corps. Here I was, a young mother with no plan, no hopes, no dreams, seeking attention, not really knowing what love was, trying to find it in all the wrong places. During my pregnancy, I started dating the man that would later be the father to my five other children. It was a good relationship at first. Then we moved in together, and I began to see a different side to him. There was the getting pushed down the steps while carrying my oldest daughter, spitting in my face, getting thrown across the room, slamming my head against the wall, getting slammed on a car, and getting kicked in my stomach while carrying our youngest daughter. Let's not even talk about the financial abuse and moving from house to house, apartment to apartment, and motel to motel. I left home at the age of seventeen to escape the abuse, but ironically, I ran right into the arms of the same abuse I had already experienced.

Fifteen more years of abuse. Why did I stay for so long? Kids? Low self-esteem? Would another man want me? Didn't think I could make it on my own? These are the main reasons, so many other women and I choose to put up with such violence. The saying goes: when you are tired of being tired, only then will you make a change. The first change I made was picking up a knife and slicing his back. He never hit me again. The second change I made was putting myself and my children on another Greyhound bus after having a gun put to my head. He said he had nothing to do with it. A few days later, he was arrested on drug charges. That was my time to run some more, to relocate again.

Savannah, Georgia, a new beginning…but was it…

Things fell into place quickly. During this transition period, I only had income tax money to work with. My godmother, who had also relocated to Savannah, allowed me and my children to live with her. I was not with her long. I was able to get a 2-bedroom apartment and later was employed by one of the biggest companies in Savannah as an Accounts Receivable Clerk. May I add I did not have any work experience in the clerical field. Things were going well. The kids and I were happy. Then husband number one was released from jail. Yes, you already know what happened next. The cycle started all over again. There was no physical abuse this time, but the mental and financial abuse was stronger than before. I lost my apartment. Money was always missing, and it seemed we were moving every six months. It took a few more years of this toxic relationship, but I finally filed divorce papers. But what pushed me to file? Was it because I finally realized that I deserved better? Was it because he was cheating? Was it because I was so fed up that I started dating someone else? Was it because I thought that someone else truly loved me?
Well, apparently, again, I didn't know what love was.

I was still married but separated while dating this person. Our relationship started out good. We first met at church, and later, he became a person that was there for my children and me as we were living in a shelter. He would pick us up and made sure we made it to work or school. I later became his secretary. He was in the ministry field. After my divorce was finalized, we were married the next week.

Before our marriage, I saw the signs, the red flags, but they were signs and flags I chose to ignore, such as flirting with other women. I placed him upon a pedestal. He was a musician and very gifted. Because I didn't know how to "keep him," I turned my whole life, what little life I had around. His career became mine. Anniversary banquets and revivals became a weekly ritual two to three times a week. Attending different churches and events with him took a toll on me. I was trying to be the best supportive minister's wife that I could be. I was trying to keep his eyes on me, prove myself to him, his family, and those who thought I wasn't good enough to be his wife.

Can I tell you how exhausting that was? I neglected my children and neglected and lost myself. He was never physically abusive, but the mental abuse behind closed doors took me to a different place. A lot of ministry wives are going through this right now. I've had the pleasure of hosting conferences and interviewing women who have hidden behind the hurt and pain of being in a marriage that looks good to others throughout the years. There is one delicate discussion I wish more women, especially those married to church leaders, would be more open to discussing. However, for some reason, it remains a secret. I had the pleasure of having a candid discussion with someone that could relate. I promised her that I would not share her real name. I am most appreciative of the fact that she has taken a step to share a piece of her story:

"My name is Mrs. Anne M., and I was married on February 14, 1998. I thought it would be forever. I was so in love, and I thought we were solid. We were happy, at least, I thought. In the beginning, I was in the church and an ordained Evangelist. My husband joined the ministry about two years after I did, and he came in on fire. I thought his joining the church was the answer to all our problems. He was the deacon of the church and our Bishop's Armor Bearer. I couldn't have been prouder of him, and his love for the Lord and ministry matched mine. We were on top of our game, and we both worked diligently in the church.

His desire to go outside our marriage was not outright. He started going into chat rooms and looking at porn. I didn't like it, but he didn't know these women. I thought it was something we could work through.

In 2004, I became sick and couldn't move around because the pain was so great. He met a woman, and the first of many women began. Each time, he was sorry, and he promised to never do it again. Each time, I forgave him because I thought he cheated because of my physical limitations. I felt I had to cover him, cover his name. I never shared what he was doing with anyone, especially at my church. I thought if I was going to stay then, I shouldn't go out telling anybody because I didn't want them to look at him in a bad light. I didn't want him viewed as a HYPOCRITE, but I became the HYPOCRITE!

He tried to cover up his infidelity, but it came a time that he just stopped. My oldest daughter went to high school, and he began seeing a woman named Miss T. He didn't bother to hide his affair, and each day, I became more broken. He announced to me that he never loved me and never would. I was devastated.

I still didn't share what was going on in my house. Then one day, I got a call from my daughter. She told me her friend (who was just 17 years old at the time) had approached her at work. She showed her a message her dad had sent her in messenger. The message was simple, "Hey beautiful, can I get a friend request." A common phrase he used to engage women on social media. I remember sitting on my bed cutting the skin off an apple with a knife. I don't remember putting the knife down. I sat numb looking at this man I vowed to love for the rest of my life, fighting back the tears and nausea. I looked for the knife because I wanted to kill him! How could you be so stupid? Did you not care what this was doing to me, our kids? I swear God himself must have removed that knife because it was no longer there.

My Apostle called me and said we would meet on Sunday after becoming aware of what happened. The meeting changed my life because now all the truth was out. I realized he didn't love me and concluded our marriage wasn't normal. Sharing the truth freed me because I was drowning and lies. The last three years of my marriage, I was extremely miserable. What we had was not healthy, and it was not in God's plan for my life. I finally concluded that I loved him, but not enough to live a lie. After spending five days with his mistress, I packed his bags and put him out. It has been almost two years, and I am finally at peace."

If you are wondering what Mrs. Anne's story has to do with this book. Well, I truly believe when one woman gets the courage to share her truth, another woman will follow. I don't know the statistics, but I believe there are women in jail due to being provoked or simply trying to defend themselves.

My two years of marriage to my second ex-husband turned into something I could never have imagined. I was accused of sleeping with his father, my boss, my co-workers. The one that hurt most was accusations of sleeping with our pastor, who gave him the keys to the church, literally. Not only was I dealing with that while trying to pretend to others that we had a perfect marriage, but there was the degrading of my children. The person I thought would be a good role model turned out to be the opposite. I don't remember the exact age, maybe 13 or 14, but one of my sons was arrested and taken to YDC (Youth Detention Center). Why? It was because of an argument that went sideways. He was provoking my son, something he had a knack at doing to all of us. Then gunshots fired, and the next thing I knew, my son was sitting in the back of a police car. The crazy thing about this day is that I told my son he had an anger issue; instead of seeing what was happening, my second husband was toxic. By no means am I saying my children were never in the wrong. Blended families are on a different level, something we didn't really talk about often. So, you're probably wondering why I didn't separate from him or file for divorce after this incident. You have to understand that I was determined to make this marriage work and get my children in line. I was going to make them respect him, no matter what. Again, trying to prove to the naysayers I was worthy and good enough to be his wife, even though I didn't speak in tongues…but that's a story for another book.

A few more months went by, the accusations were getting worse. I dealt with him paying for another female's hotel room. I overlooked that he was having "prayer meetings" with other women. Other things started to happen. He took my name off our joint checking account and later closed it. Here I am, thinking the bills were being paid. Remember I told you I was naïve. The hotel female's late-night phone calls and text messages came like clockwork. But yet again, I was determined to make our marriage work. I don't see how that was possible, considering we never prayed or read the Word together. It is safe to say God was nowhere near or in our marriage.

This particular day started out as any normal day, at least in my eyes. We were invited to attend a graduation ceremony for those incarcerated who had turned their lives around. I had no idea that I would find myself sitting in the back of a police car by the end of this night and later taken to jail. When we arrived home after work, the electricity had been cut off. We decided to make a night of it after the ceremony and get a hotel room. The children spent the night at the neighbors, and we went to the event.

I enjoyed listening to those sharing their testimony of overcoming and putting in the work to change. It was a wonderful experience, and I truly did not want to leave. After the graduation was over, we proceeded to the hotel. He went in to pay. Then I intercepted a text message asking him, "Where he was and why he was with me?" I began to read other messages of them texting back and forth. As he got back in the car, I never gave him a chance to say anything. I just started hitting and punching him, tears flowing, yelling, cursing, and screaming at him. He lied to me.

The trust had been broken. He told me a couple weeks prior he had stopped seeing her. He pushed a button, and anger took over. I was out of control. I begged him to take me home. As I got out of the truck, she called, and he had the audacity to talk to her right in front of my face. He told her I was acting crazy. I grabbed the phone from him, and she was laughing. The next few words that came out of her mouth just took me over the edge. "You can put him out, and he can come live with me at the hotel." I gave him the phone back, he got out of the truck, and I just sat there for a few minutes. I went inside the house, to the kitchen and grabbed a knife, he ran. I got back into my truck. I sat there in disbelief. After everything, I did for him. The way he treated my kids and me, the accusations, were the thoughts that ran through my mind. All this time, he was the one cheating, a minister. I glanced up, and he was walking towards the truck. He was still talking to her. I asked him to hang up so we could talk. He didn't. He said he needed to talk to her instead.

By this time, I just wanted to leave, but as I drove off and looked in the rear-view mirror, I could see him still on the phone and laughing. I snapped. I made a U-turn in our yard and, BOOM! It happened so fast. I saw him duck behind a tree stump, at least I thought. When I stopped the truck and got out, I didn't see him. I thought he ran. I stood there for a few minutes, wondering what in the hell just happened and thinking I needed help with my own anger issues. I went into the house to grab some clothes. I just wanted to get away and collect my thoughts. As I approached the other side of the truck, my heart stopped. The truck…well, I actually drugged him a few feet, and I honestly did not realize it. I saw the blood. He was going in and out of consciousness, and she was still on the phone. I heard her calling his name. I hung up and called 911. I called one of my good friends who lived a few minutes away and said I believe I killed my husband. It seemed to of taken forever for the ambulance to get there. I kept trying to wake him up. I kept apologizing to him. The ambulance and my family friend arrived at the same time. The look on their faces said it all. He was dying. Then there was the silence. I could see their lips moving, but I couldn't hear anything. I was standing there in a daze. It was like a scene from a movie. I could see the different facial expressions, disbelief, shock, and concern, as I looked around. The look of the EMS workers who put him in the back of the ambulance told me he wasn't going to survive.

The car ride to the jail seemed to have taken hours, but it was only a few minutes. I kept replaying in my head what had happened. The officer that was driving was very sympathetic to me. She even shed some tears. She talked about the many women behind bars due to domestic violence as we drove. She tried to prepare me for what was to come. She told me to stay strong and that I would be okay. As we approached the jail, she told me she would have to put the handcuffs on me. She said, "I trust you, and I know you are not going to do anything crazy." It felt like I was going crazy. As she began to walk me inside, another officer came up to us and said additional charges would be added. I for sure thought he was going to say homicide. Instead, it was aggravated assault and aggravated battery. I could breathe a little.

Questions on top of questions. Different detectives. My mind was gone. I couldn't think, and I was scared. I was praying he was okay. I was later told he was in ICU. It was then I realized what I had been afraid to admit. I had a huge problem; ANGER. It was an issue that stemmed from childhood abuse. Over time, I became my adoptive mother. I was out of control, and it wasn't the first time. I hid behind this one barrier for years: me, the abusee, became the abuser.

Abuse..this thing that set the course

Abuse..this thing that said I wasn't worthy

Abuse..this thing that said no one would love me

Abuse..this thing that tore my life apart

Glory to God, he was given a second chance to live. I was given a second chance to live.

Two things happened on this day. First, I realized the enemy does come to kill, steal, and destroy. I experienced, not the first time within this marriage, how the enemy could come in within minutes and disrupt or change the course of events. As we were both "in the church," neither one of us took the time to ask God to intervene in this situation. Even when I first realized he was cheating, I never consulted God, never prayed. Secondly, I witnessed and experienced both GRACE and MERCY. What the enemy definitely meant for bad, God said no. The husband shall live (physically), and you shall live spiritually were the words I heard while in the holding cell.

"Bend over and cough," not the words that a naïve country girl should hear. But this is how I got here.

The next few days in lock-up were and still is a blur. The day before my bond hearing, my public defender, an officer, and a few inmates told me the judge that was seeing me never gave a bond, and I would be there until my court date, which would be anywhere between 30 and 90 days. I cried, I cried, I cried. Jail life was not for me. It's amazing how God will go before you and speak on your behalf. That same judge that never gave a bond gave it to me, and I was released. Maybe it was because I had six children. Maybe it was because that was the first time ever being in trouble. Maybe it was because the officers could go back and look at the text messages from him and the hotel female. I know for a fact it was all God.

My court date arrived. The sentence was eight years' probation, restitution fines, and community service under The First Offenders Act, which refers to a person convicted of a legal offense for the first time. A lot of people couldn't believe it. Some thought I should have been put under the jail. I know for a fact that it was all God.

Some felt my 8-year probation sentence was a slap on the wrist, but that was actually the worst eight years of my life. Trying to recover all I had lost, my home, my job, my mind. I was working on restoring my joy, my peace, my brokenness. What's more, even after he got out of the hospital, I tried to restore my marriage. Seriously, who in the world in their right mind would want to go back to the person that almost took their life. Toxic! But in my defense, he said that he wanted to work things out. I went to rehab with him. We started praying together. But when my back was turned, I was the cray-cray B…Toxic!!

So, we divorced in 2011. Hallelujah! A fresh and new start. Another chance to focus and to get myself together and to restore the broken relationship I thought I caused between my children and myself. What is the cost of having another chance?

There were dark days. I was unemployed, cried a lot, depressed, and ashamed. I had suicidal thoughts, and truthfully, I tried to end it all by taking a handful of pills. I had no career goals. Here I go again, proving myself. I had to prove that I was not that evil person who committed that ultimate sin. I tried to do things and get involved with people who could ease and hide my emotional and spiritual pain. The enemy was really in my head. I felt I wasn't worthy enough to be in the presence of God. It got to the point where I didn't want to go outside, to the grocery store or church. I felt as though everyone was watching and talking about me. I felt like somebody knew me and knew what I had done no matter where I went. I always felt compelled to tell what happened, to tell my side of the story. The "church" saints took his side, but who took my side? Who was fighting for me? I was condemning myself. However, I can tell you, about three months after the incident, no one even cared about what took place. It wasn't even talked about. No one even remembered. It was my own thoughts that were causing the confusion in my mind. I judged my-self.

It took me ten years to write this part of my story. I share my testimony, so you will not do what I did. It has taken many years to free myself. I can now share my whole truth without crying and knowing God has delivered and forgiven me. And guess what? I have forgiven myself, the ex-husbands, and my mother that inflicted so much turmoil in my life. But the best part of this is being able to go through the redemption process.

About a year ago, I was on Facebook and watched a video. The video is about a father dancing with his daughter at her school's father-daughter dance. It was the way she looked at him, the way he looked at her, the smiles, and the hugs. Tears began to roll down my face, not sad tears, but tears of joy. It was at this time I finally felt like I was truly redeemed. At this moment, I knew my life mattered and that God had a plan and a purpose for me. There was a time this father, my ex, was lying in an ICU bed fighting for his life. Praises to the Most High God. He is a God of first, second, and third chances.

Here is an important fact I want everyone that reads this book to know. It took some time, but I had to hold myself accountable for my actions. I did not have the right to harm or inflict pain on anyone else. At first, I tried to blame him, the first husband, and even my adoptive mother. As time went on, I realized I never got the proper help I needed for my anger. I took counseling classes here and there. I attended for a few days, then stopped once I felt as though I was better. My eight-year probation period was a time for me to get myself together mentally. This is what I needed because I had been on a path of destruction.

No, I was not incarcerated months or years like so many others. I'm inclined to share; I was arrested right before the end of my probationary period due to a mix-up with paperwork. My ten days in jail hit differently. I had an up-close-and-personal encounter with those that had been in for over five years, some longer. Some lives were broken. Some boldly shared how they got to that place of feeling like life had beat them down to the core. I witnessed the beautiful drawings from a young lady who loved art. I listened to the voice of an angel as she sang a worship song. It appears; worship was all she had left. Even though I tried to keep to myself, some asked me to pray for and with them. They shared their hopes and dreams with me, at least the ones that still had a dream. They made promises to turn their lives around if given the opportunity. As the 4th of July weekend was approaching, I had no idea how long I would be there. On the 10th day, I called my daughter for a ride. I left knowing there was plenty of work that needed to be done. How can one's value be restored? How can one rise above rejection after rejection?

I can sympathize and empathize with them. I know all too well what it feels like to beg for a job and a decent place to live. I will never forget the day I scheduled an interview with one of the top staffing agencies in Savannah. My resume was on point, and I nailed the interview. Things were finally looking up. However, the interview ended with me getting off the elevator in tears and coming to the realization my name would be removed from their database due to my felony charge. In a short time, the side hustles became the new norm. Whew!! I didn't know I was good at hustling (in a good way). Let's say that survival mood was taken to a whole new level.

I remember paying hundreds of dollars on application fees to find housing only to get denied in return. I remember begging for help and trying my best to explain why I had a criminal background to landlords or housing agencies.

As I reflect upon the many conversations I had with other felons and advocates, there is one word we all can agree on —Change. How do we change the laws that will give us access to programs that deny us due to felony charges? How do we apply for an office job without being judged or denied because of a mistake? How do we submit applications for housing when no one will give us a chance? These are only a few of the changes that can be made, but who is willing to make them?

I changed. Other convicted felons changed. When does the system truly change?

Keya Jest

Savannah native who survived the trenches of the streets is Keya Jest. After almost twenty years of active addiction, I decided to want a new way to live on January 28, 2014. After entering the program Chatham Apprentice and enrolling into Step of Savannah, I began to flourish into a productive member of society. This program built my confidence by being labeled a convicted felon and receiving no's for employment. It taught me how to keep my head held high. It also provided me with resume building and connected me to Consumer Crediting to fix my credit. It provided counseling and legal services to help remove charges off my background. Among other avenues of help through this program, it helped me up to be a success. I received a higher-paying full-time job with benefits because of this program. After being nominated for the Step Up Board of Directors, I accepted it with honor in 2017. United Way of Coastal Georgia played a huge part in my return to society after being homeless and experiencing active addiction. United way fed me, clothed me, helped me get my social security card and birth certificate. I was featured as one of "Savannah's Own Success Stories" at United Way's Giving Campaign.

The doors for interviews began to flourish for me in 2017. WSAV, WTOC, Bounce T.V., and Savannah Tribune interviewed me. I also had two radio interviews locally to share my testimony. Chatham Living Magazine wrote an article about me and how I survived the streets in 2019.

Today, I am a local recording artist, and I use music and lyrics to talk about my struggles about where I've been. I returned to school and received my Associates degree in Business Management. Now, I'm an Undergraduate pursuing my Masters in social work. I'm also a Peer Specialist who helps assist rehabilitation, mental health, and substance abuse clients in a crisis center. If anyone needs a motivational speaker, I am willing to share my story, uncut, in all truth. You can email me at Keya.Jest@gmail.com or call (912)237-2357 for speaking engagements.

✟ Rock Bottom to Rock Solid ✟

My name is Keya Jest. I'm in long-term recovery with close to eight years clean and serene. I've joined with other recovering addicts and alcoholics worldwide in my process. They have been my strong support system. I am clinically diagnosed with depression, anxiety, and PTSD. I'm actively engaged with treatment plans with my therapist and function levelheaded in society on the mental health side. I am a convicted felon, and although I can't change my past, I have proved to be a productive member of society today.

In this chapter, I'm going to give you insight into the life I lived before I became a convicted felon, my life while I was a convicted felon, and how I rose above the stigma of my issues and became one of "Savannah's Own Success Story."

I decided to write a chapter in this book because I feel there's a calling on my life to share my testimony. I want to give hope to the hopeless and help those with dreams that have died to help reawaken them. My desire is to help the reader find their purpose and live out their dreams. Don't allow anything to hold you back. It's the push that birth's purpose. I need the reader to understand that many people make bad decisions throughout life; some are remorseful, and some are not. I found the remorseful ones have made great efforts to change the course of their lives. Here's a thought, try telling someone strung out on crack to be a good citizen, don't steal this or that, and stop putting yourself in high-risk situations. Will they listen? Eventually, individuals will come around ONLY if they want a new way of life with a conscience. However, before that change, their Integrity goes out the door. There's no conscience on how others are treated, and the law isn't respected. This is a hard truth, but I must keep it real. No one wants to be in the grip of a dog bite, right? This is the best way to explain my story. I was caught in the grip...I was caught in the grips of homelessness, drug abuse, prostitution, and a criminal life-style. I didn't value myself, and I often felt like giving up on life. The more I tried to shake it off, I couldn't until God stepped in and changed me. There is life above crime. There's a beautiful life when you're able to live in the confidence of not breaking the law. It's a beautiful feeling when there are no warrants for your arrest hanging over your head. However, My substance addiction had me in places I never would've gone clean and serene. This is my story:

No human power was strong enough to break the bondage that held me bound in addiction. NONE! I was homeless on the streets of Savannah by choice. I say that because I had a home to go to, but because I wanted to live in the streets to do what I wanted to do, I lived away from my mom's house. I decided to clean up my act on January 28, 2014. That's my clean date! That was the day that I made a conscious decision to walk away from the streets. I left behind a lifestyle of substance abuse, prosti-tution, and crime. Even though it's been close to eight years, my back-ground check can still be used to dictate my character. I've grown to understand that God has a unique and definite plan for my life. God was and still is in charge of my life. What is meant for me will be, and the closed doors did not stop me from becoming greater.

As I stated, I am a convicted felon. My charges were in Chatham County, Savannah, Georgia, and Gwinnett County in Norcross, Georgia. My first arrest was nine counts of forgery in Savannah, Georgia. I was able to get First Offenders since I was never in trouble before. When I traveled to Norcross at the height of my addiction, I had numerous misdemeanor charges. Once I returned to Savannah, I caught a sale case where I received ten years' probation.

Before I share my accomplishments, I want to walk you through my life before my convictions and during. I must say, I am proud of myself and give God all of the Praise. I couldn't have done anything without him. Who would've thought? An addict like me, who survived the trenches of the streets, would be a productive member of society. I'm full of gratitude today, knowing my second chance at life was worth fighting for. Every time I went to jail, my addiction played a part in it. The first time I ever used it was...so let's back up to 1992.

I graduated from Savannah High School. It was one of the happiest days of my life! I did it! All those days of schoolwork, exams, waking up early mornings finally paid off! My classmates didn't know I hid two pregnancies, resulting in abortions. This type of news was unexpected from a sweet, quiet girl who never got in trouble. This was the turning point in my life where I would begin to spiral downward mentally. I was emotionally distraught and scared of becoming a mother. Out of fear and with no support, I decided to have abortions. Imagine making that type of decision twice in high school! I went through the procedures and continued my life wounded, broken, ashamed, and feeling guilty. This is where my depression began.

Then I entered college at Georgia Southern University. I remember in high school looking through a catalog and seeing what careers paid well. I decided to Major in Computer Science. That didn't end well because I dropped out after a few months of being there. I was interested in the relationship I got involved with and wanted to spend more time with him. This became another downward spiral because of drug use. I've witnessed many who smoked marijuana and drank alcohol, so this behavior didn't seem bad. It wouldn't become a problem to the point of being addicted; I would coach myself into believing. I was in a circle of people who used and went to work. If they can cope and maintain a stable life, I can too.

At that time, I realized I wasn't looking out of a clear lens. I only witnessed what I wanted to witness. Yes, they kept jobs and a roof over their head, but what was happening behind the scenes? Have their lives become unmanageable over time? As I began to rationalize and justify entering into the lifestyle of drugs, my thoughts were always, "it's not a big deal." However, that mindset dug me deeper into a lifestyle of drugs and criminal acts. Before things got worse in my life, I wanted to enlist in the army. This was after I failed at finishing college. I went to the MEPS station in Florida and was turned around. I used marijuana for the first time in my life just before traveling down. To clean your system from testing positive, I needed to drink vinegar. I brought a bottle of vinegar and drank as much as I could on my way to the MEPS Station. When I got there and took the physical, I didn't pass. In fact, the vinegar gave me a bladder infection. I left Florida more depressed. I thought to myself, where's the career move? I'm failing and spiraling.

As time went on, drugs and alcohol became more than recreation. It was a necessity. I couldn't function without it. I couldn't keep a job while on it, and I found out my money would run out fast when I purchased it. This is where the road of destruction began. This is where I was introduced to handcuffs and officers, patty wagons and bookings, attorneys, D.A.'s, and Judges. I also met hardened criminals, murderers, and pimps. All I wanted was to get high. I did not care about a felony on my record or a jail sentence. Whatever was needed to be done to get high, I just about did it all. I was out of my mind and did not care about the consequences. This season of my life resulted from me smoking crack. How did I start? I had a great job, my first apartment, and a puppy named Cookie. One evening, I came home, calculated my bills, and found out I was still short for my utilities after paying rent. Understanding this, I decided I wanted to sell crack. I knew enough to go find it in the hood and flip it to make more money. I watched someone closely one evening about a year prior make plays. He would ride, slang, and collect. He was like, look, sis! As he spread a knot of money in his hand. I was impressed. I reacted from that planted seed and went to the westside to get a pack of dope. After being fluked the first time, losing $50, I made a second attempt. This run was successful. I did get what I wanted, but I couldn't sell it. I threw the towel in after an old head grabbed what he wanted out of the pack when I showed him what I had for sale. I came home frustrated. I placed the remainder of the pack on the TV and stared at it. I wondered how it would make me feel if I tried it. I was in a relationship at the time, and he responded, "if you try it, then I would." So, I tried it. The best feeling of my life immediately came and went. This is where hell broke loose. I chased that same high that I will never get again. To be real, I wished my boyfriend at the time would've put his foot down when I shared my thought of using. I used to blame him for not stepping up and talking me out of it. Today I understand I made a choice. I regret not setting a boundary for him. I should have told him no, just like I wished he would have done for me. I should've had more love for him, not allowing him to slip. I brought it home and immediately tore the house down.

Ladies, I want to remind you that we have power over some men. We all should be vessels that will build and not tear down. Eventually, I walked off my job after tearing down the house (imagine an explosion going off and trying to maneuver through the rubble and smoke). Cookie was my first pet, but I neglected her while in active addiction then eventually took her to the pound. My first apartment became the crack house quickly! Things got so bad I decided to move away to Jacksonville, Florida. I felt if I changed demographics, I could stop smoking dope. I left for

Jacksonville by pawning a local rent-to-own TV. I got the money and brought my ticket. I got on the bus with my boyfriend at the time and headed to Jacksonville. I felt God was with me because it was one bed open for me when I got there. The staff said I was lucky. I knew it was an act of God. I remember only having $20 left in my pocket. I stayed at the homeless shelter for a few days until I found a cleaning job at a hotel. I found a local church and began seeking God heavily. Before I began using, a woman literally begged me to get saved. I kept making excuses about how I couldn't make it to church. Suddenly, people were hitting me up with coming to church, be my guest here, be my guest there. It was like a flood of church requests. I felt God was trying to tell me something. I found out years later why. He knocked so I could answer. To this day, I'm glad I answered. I answered by visiting a local church in Savannah and got saved.

At this time, I felt like my life was beginning to get back on track, and it did. I cleaned rooms playing my gospel music, praying God would use me as a vessel. I told God wherever he tells me to go, I'll go. I can recall the puffy eyes and the snot running down my lips from my nose. I was sincere, and I was willing.

After this prayer, maybe about a week or two later, I was back using. I could not understand how something like this could happen. How can I get saved, ask God into my heart, and begin to use crack? It didn't sit well with me. I was angry at God and believed He didn't love me. Didn't He see the tears I cried? Didn't He examine my heart for sincerity? I learned that it doesn't matter where you go; drugs will be found. I also learned I could've said no. My boyfriend at the time found the drugs not too far from the hotel. Can you believe this? Lesson learned: A relationship involving drugs will not work if you both aren't on the same page. Both have to want to stop using. I was off to the races once again, this time in a city I knew nothing about.

During this season, entering into active addiction, I pursued a career in music as a recording rap artist in Savannah. This was before I left for Jacksonville. I started slacking writing lyrics, and I was embarrassed that I became a "crackhead." I knew I wouldn't get any respect from my hometown, seeing me strung out on the streets and trying to be a rap artist. The day I decided to return home, my boyfriend and I contacted the producer and asked him to come get us from Jacksonville. Here I go once again, running from my drug use. My hotel room became the crack room, and I had to abandon another animal, which was a kitten.

Upon returning to Savannah, I spiraled fast. I knew where the crack houses were on either side of town. I knew how to steal and not get caught to get another hit, or so I thought. I remember linking up with a mastermind who was able to help me get more dope to smoke. All I had to do was use a fake I.D. with my personal pic, sign a fake signature that matched the name on the I.D., and collect the money from the establishments. The risk was jail time, and of course, each establishment had cameras, so eventually, I would get caught. Most of the time, I went in cracked out, fidgeting, and with my eyes buck wild. Mastermind promised me $50 out each check I cashed. That was $50 out of almost an $800 lick. From a fiend's perspective, I was ballin'. I remember stepping onto the club scene after collecting from a few runs. Of course, I coped my dope before heading out. By this time in my addiction, I couldn't function without it.

I was used to crack houses, abandon houses, lanes, and trap houses. But for once, in my addiction, I wanted to be normal. I wanted to experience the lifestyle of the streets in the club. I had at least $300 in my pocket. You couldn't tell me anything. Let's celebrate and buy a bottle of Moet, I said to a companion at the time who went out with me. By the end of the night, when I realized I could've spent that money on crack instead of a drink, I was furious! Couldn't believe the stupidity. I tried to live life outside of smoking dope for a brief moment, but it didn't last long. Dope always won.

There was a time I wanted to get another puppy and got one. A random puppy out the hood was roaming the streets, like me. I took the puppy in and named it. I wanted to rekindle a relationship with another animal, knowing I had always abandoned them in the past. I felt as if I was a little more responsible even though it was obvious, I was strung out and barely homeless. I lived in a rooming house on the west side of Savannah with a steady income from my prostitution profession. As fast as it came in, I smoked it all up. After bringing her to my crack-infested room, I decided she must go to the vet for shots. I walked her to the Veterinarian on Bull street and found out she had worms and was forced to pay for her care. I knew I had to be responsible. I left the vet cradling her with love, but at the same time, I was angry for spending my dope money. I brought her first bag of dog food from the nearest store and fixed her a bowl. I felt the monkey on my back and wanted to get some dope. I took the remainder of the dog food back to the store for a refund. My excuse, the dog, didn't like it. The thirst was real when I wanted to use. The first item I can remember selling while in the streets was a light bulb. I took the light bulb out of the light fixture and caught a couple of young dope boys in the lane. I showed them what I had, and they almost beat me down. They cussed me out and told me to stay away. They said I "tried them." What you don't do is bring heat to the dope boys, and that's what I did by having them meet me in a lane thinking I'm about to purchase but pulled out a light bulb instead. These actions were called "junkie moves" in the streets.

As for my new puppy, once again, I abandoned it. I couldn't pay for rent and lost everything I owned. This time I left everything in the rooming house, including the puppy. I went back in the streets homeless and found myself smoking from pillow to post.

There're many stories I can share while I was in active addiction. They all proved a point; my addiction was getting the best of me. I had no idea how cutthroat the streets were. That caring, timid, fragile woman had to step her game up to survive. I remember an older woman who was also strung out told me I needed to have the devil in my eye. I was confused as to why she would warn me in that manner. I thought to myself, the devil in my eye??

As time went on, as I began to trim around on Savannah's west side, I began to understand what she meant. The men I would meet would hang around me like vultures. I always thought they were cool, that they were protecting me, but it turned out they were waiting on me to make my money and cope. I was kind-hearted, so I didn't mind sharing my drugs or money, but that quickly changed. Many things were done by me in the streets I wasn't proud of. I always felt like if I got to the point of putting myself on the market for cash to use dope, it would be the lowest I could go. Jumping in and out of cars was scary at times. I never knew who I was with in the car. I wondered how I became comfortable yet uncomfortable with exchanging sex for money. I thought about my childhood and realized I was introduced to prostitution very young. When I was younger, my dad and mom worked full-time, and I was forced to stay with a babysitter. This was when I experienced being molested. I was molested by the babysitter's daughter, who had to be a high school student at the time. I kept this a secret until my adult years because I was embarrassed. You always hear about males molesting females, not females molesting females.

During my healing process and being four years clean and serene, I began looking back into my life with a microscope. I realized I was introduced to prostitution by the female's daughter and realized I was experiencing addiction early. This was her tactic. She bought candy for me each day and kept it on her dresser until nightfall. Once everyone was sound asleep, she would offer the candy to me only if she could touch me or I touch her. I didn't think this was wrong. I wasn't taught about good touch bad touch like I see today. Besides, my mom kept me from candy. She didn't want me getting cavities. Candy became the drug for me. I remember taking money out of my mom's purse and went to the corner store for candy. The young lady brought me home, told my mom what I was doing, and handed her the $100 bill. At this young age, I experienced addiction and found ways and means to get more. As an adult, I found ways to pay for my drugs. It was a very expensive habit. It cost me my freedom, relationships, my dignity, and finances. It was never enough money to pay for my drugs.

Let me take you to the height of my addiction. Eventually, I stopped prostituting on Jefferson street and began staying in hotel rooms on Ogeechee Road, Hwy 17 in Savannah, Ga. When I got on 17, I was told to be successful out there, get a room, some dope, and find a female who was already out there prostituting. I brought a wooden handle gun off someone living in one of the hotels. I never shot a gun in my life, let alone loading bullets. I got a pack of dope and found someone to join my team. That situation didn't last long. Eventually, I was approached by a pimp who asked me to join him so he could buy me under clothes. I told him I could buy my own and walked off. Due to making this area my stomping grounds, I was beaten with a pistol and hit across my head with a bottle for selling dope to one of the plays that weren't mine. Officers came out to the call and asked me what I was doing on 17. I didn't belong. I didn't have an answer, and they were right. I wanted to leave and go to Atlanta;

maybe try another demographic while using was a constant thought. This was another level of the streets that caused me to become angry, bitter, and ready to do whatever was needed to survive. Prostituting became a little easier, I mostly stayed in the rooms, and the tricks found me. One day I made the decision to leave Savannah and head to Atlanta. I was a newbie in the place I ended up.

My first stop was Lawrenceville, Ga. I stole a van to get there. On Hwy 17, some addicts would pawn their vehicles for drugs. A young man got stuck in the hotel. Stuck, meaning he spent all his money. His drugs were gone, and he was sitting waiting on his vehicle to return. I remember the guy saying he couldn't call the cops on the dope boy who had his vehicle. Evidently, he couldn't let his family know his whereabouts and what he had been doing all week. The guy and I stayed in the same room that week, waiting for the return of his van. The day the dope boy left with the van, I got robbed from them. I had a couple of hundred dollars hidden in an old suitcase. We were rolling dice, and I kept reaching in the bag sneakily to bet money. That's where I messed up. A lesson I've learned on the streets is that we all looked for a "come up." When the opportunity presented itself, it was good as gone. I grabbed more money and headed out the door. When I got back, the dope boy was gone along with my money. I was furious. I was sick of Savannah and the tricks I met during this time. I was totally ready to leave. I believe the last straw was when I let someone hear my recorded music on a CD, and that person broke it in half and gave it back to me. I had an extra copy. If I went to Atlanta, I felt I may have a better chance of survival and having my music heard from Big Execs.

One night to my surprise, the dope boy came back with the van; however, the owner wasn't there. In fact, the owner said forget the van, he had to return home. I never knew what happened to the guy, but I took his van.

I also robbed that same dope boy that robbed me. He came into the room and fell asleep. I got my suitcase and headed to Atlanta. Before I nervously opened the room door to exit, something said to grab the guy's shoes. I grabbed the shoes and left. I pulled the tongue out of one shoe and found a couple hundred dollars. The dope boy and I broke even. I got my money back. Some of the stunts I pulled while in active addiction could've ended my life.

After taking different paths throughout the years, committing multiple crimes, and learning hardcore lessons, I finally made it back to Savannah. However, my using continued. I was paranoid from the licks I pulled while in the streets. I didn't know if they knew I was back. This time around, strolling on Jefferson and locked in crack houses, I began to talk to God. Someone told me, "Acknowledge God in all my ways, and he shall direct my path." I thought to myself, "All my ways?" Even in active addiction? So, I began to talk to God, walking, praying with a pipe in my hand. Then I began to meet people in the hood that would come out to use but had a message of hope for me. Believe it or not, God was speaking. Or was God always speaking, but I never acknowledged him? One day a woman asked could she pray for me. I reached out my hand and said yes. I believe this is the most powerful part of my story. This lady grabbed my hand for prayer! My fingers were black and dirty, I hadn't washed in days, and she looked past that in love to pray for me! She was a block from the dope house and always watched the traffic from her porch. After that prayer, people began kicking me out of their houses, with or without money. The doors kept closing. The more I strolled, the more the cars would pass by me. God began intervening more to get me off the streets.

I remember one Sunday morning; I was on the block for hours. Cars passed by me, but none stopped. I began to feel starving hunger pains. I saw a guy at the corner store and asked him to buy me something to eat. He told me to get what I wanted. I picked out two hotdogs and two bags of chips, costing around $3.00. The guy brought the food, but he carried it in his hand. He told me to follow him to his place. I'm following with no questions asked. I reached his apartment, went inside, sat down, and he gave me the food. Then he asked, "What are you going to do for it?" Keep in mind, I'm starving. I thought to myself, it's food…turn the trick. Then all of a sudden, anger built in me. I yelled at him and told him he was trifling! I yelled, "How you gone try me up, sex for a $3.00 meal?" I left without having sex, and I took my food. I always think of that day. I came close to selling myself for two hotdogs and two bags of chips.

January 28, 2014, was the day I decided to get off the streets. On January 01, 2014, I sat outside the crack house, going into the new year. It was 11:45pm the night prior; I was busted with no cash and disgusted because I didn't want to sell myself to use. I watched drug fiends go into the dope house, and I became furious. No one invited me up. There's no southern hospitality in the dope game. I remember praying in the new year. I remember asking God to cover me and to help me quit using. I begged, "please help me." In the same breath, I jumped up and began strolling the blocks. A car pulled up, and I got in. He took me near a cemetery at a park that faced HWY 17. I was going to handle my business. He thought this would be a normal sex-for-money transaction, but I jumped out of the car and walked inside the park. He ran behind me and choked me. He was trying to pull my pants off but couldn't because he was choking me. He choked me so bad that I urinated on myself and passed out. I came too, still feeling the squeeze of his muscle to my windpipe. I couldn't scream. I was losing consciousness. What happened next was an act of God. A police car road down HWY 17, and I pointed at it. It shook him, and he let go. He gave a strong punch to the face and left. I cried all the way to the dope spot and still wanted to use. Did I call the police? No, sadly, I didn't. All I cared about was getting high.

Guess what happened next? I left the scene shook and eventually started to walk the streets again. A few weeks later, I jumped in a different car, but it was the same guy. This time it was daylight, and he took me inside the graveyard to handle business. Immediately afterward, when he jumped out of the car and ran to my side of the car yelling, I recognized the sound of his voice. I began to recognize the complexion of his skin and the tattoos. I couldn't believe I did not recognize the guy. When the guy was finished robbing me and beating me, he jumped in his car. I could hear him laugh as he blew the horn. That horn when it blew, I read it as being I got you again.

A couple of years prior, I jumped into a car and was held at gunpoint. I can go on and on about how the streets came close to taking my life and how God showed up and covered me. This was when I decided to make a change. I couldn't recognize my attacker. I was just that strung out. My mind was gone. I felt like I would get killed in the streets if I didn't change my life. One night, at 3 AM, I was walking down the street, and a guy walked on the side of me trying to hold a conversation. As I continued with him, my mind told me, "cross the street, now!" That was the first time I ever experienced my thoughts yelling at me. Immediately, I went to cross the street. As I walked across the street of Martin Luther King Blvd, the guy ran up and grabbed me from behind. When I turned to look in his face, his teeth, facial structure, and ears looked demonic. He dragged me across the four lanes of traffic until he got me on the side of an abandoned building, and he tried to take my pants off. He got them to my ankles. I heard a woman yelling, "Leave her alone!" Within moments I was around the corner, hugging the stop sign with my pants down to my ankle. The attacker walked up to me and punched me in the face, then ran off.

I constantly think about how God covered me throughout my addiction, and I have to shout Hallelujah!! There's a praise in my dance and a praise in my new walk of life. I was counted out when I desired to be counted in. It was God who thought highly of me to block death when it knocked on my door. My first few years of recovery were challenging. I'd fill out job applications I desired and was honest about my criminal background but was denied.

At one point, I got so discouraged I stopped filling out applications because I heard the no before I even tried. After completing the Chatham Apprentice Program, I regained my confidence. Every job I applied for that I wanted since this program I received. Now, I'm walking in my purpose. I'm able to give back to a community that I once wounded and help those who suffer from mental illness and addiction. I see myself repeatedly in these individuals, and I can help with empathy and compassion.

As a convicted felon, I accepted that title. I can't change the past, but I will not let a title cripple me. There will always be judgmental folks in the world, and I came to grips with that. I know who I am today, and I know the blessing of God's grace. I realize everybody will not understand my past and think I should've gotten it together much sooner and understood my realities and consequences. I get it. This was my process. I thank God for my process. I thank God for my 2nd chance almost 20 years later.

I thank God for my new life and how He covered me. I thank God found me worthy of a second chance. That power that broke those chains came from God. He gets all the praise! Today as I look back on my life, I'm proud. All I had to do was make up my mind to be a productive member of society and take a step in that direction. I have almost eight years clean and have volunteered in different areas to give back to the community. I work for what I want today. I even held two jobs at a time to make sure ends were met. Since I got clean, I never have compromised my body for money. In fact, I am saving myself for the husband God has prepared for me. I have not been in trouble with the law since 2012.

Although legally, I am a convicted felon, I am reformed. As Savannah's Own Success Story, I had the opportunity to be interviewed by Savannah Tribune. The article was published on July 26, 2017, and it was called Keya Jest: Turning The Tide. WTOC channel 11, Larry Silbermann, shared part of my story on November 13, 2017, when I was one of the clients featured by United Way campaign. I was interviewed by Zeel Real on WRUU local radio station. I was a part of Chatham County Living Magazine- Fall 2020. Chatham County Living Magazine spring 2021 featured my story "Street Survivor" on pages 68-74. Courtney Cole interviewed me on WSAV published November 10, 2017, and described how charitable giving helped me with my homelessness process. WTOC Bounce T.V, Ms. Dawn Baker, interviewed me in 2017 also. God has opened doors for me to share my story. It takes me back to that day when I cried in the hotel room, asking God to use me as a vessel. He did and still is! My suffering wasn't in vain. It's God's power through our testimony that saves lives!

James Hicks, Jr.

James Edward Hicks Jr. was born on June 30th, 1973, at Holy Cross Hospital in Silversprings, Maryland, and raised in a small city in North Carolina called Goldsboro. I am one of three siblings and the only son.

For the most part, both my father and mother were in my life. They divorced when I was in the third grade. I grew up quite happy and energetic as a child. My imagination was extremely vivid, and I often dreamed dreams of becoming famous and exceptional in life. I never envisioned being some type of actor or entertainer. My dreams were about doing something to make a difference in people's lives. As I grew older, those dreams formulated into me desiring to be one of three things, an artist, architect, or musician. From the fifth grade until graduation, I played in some type of band. My primary instrument was and still is the trumpet. I learned how to play the saxophone, the clarinet, the baritone, and a little of the drums, or as it is properly called "percussions."

Those occupational desires eventually decreased by one. Being an artist was no longer a desire for me by high school. I took two years of architectural and mechanical drafting and fell in love with it. But the architectural drafting drew my attention more, and I favored it over the mechanical. I really wanted to design my own home. This may be something that I pursue later in life because I still have this dream.

Music is still a passion of mine. I enjoy all genres of music, from gospel to rock; jazz to symphonic; country to blues. It's something about music that just cleanses the soul. I enjoy the music, but I enjoy the words as well. It inspires me to see how people express their pain, joy, sorrow, struggles and overcome life's struggles. My love for music comes from the many different types of music I played growing up in the various bands I was a member of. Bands like the symphonic band, pep band, jazz band, and marching band all played a part in my musical development.

I graduated from high school in June of 1991. I joined the U.S. Army in November of the same year. My time in the military was a tumultuous one. Consequently, one of the stages in my life was needed to provide me with a sense of discipline and purpose. I served in the military for four years and eight months. I was released under a General Discharge under Honorable Conditions. Frankly, I was a good soldier while on duty. When I was off duty, I just couldn't find the balance between discipline and fun. For some reason, I viewed the military through the eyes of a civilian. I mean that I felt like whatever I did during my personal time was my business alone. I never understood I was on duty 24 hours a day, even if I was not in uniform.

I really enjoyed my time in the military, and the truth be told, I was sad and depressed when I was kicked out. I left behind many friends and a way of life that I was exposed to right out of high school. I didn't know any other way of seeing life or living life outside of a military point of view. Even to this day, I am military in many ways that I think and view society at large. It has been toned down and blended with civilian life to infuse the best of both worlds.

I reside in Memphis, TN, with my loving wife and stepdaughter. I have three children: a son and daughter from a prior marriage and another son from a relationship before my first marriage. I spend my days working and educating the youth about the effects of chasing illicit and illegal money. I encourage the youth to work "9 to 5 jobs" and tell them that this is the true gain in life.

I have developed a program entitled Functional Men or "FM" that teaches men of all ages to function as men. Many of us like to say a male is not a man because of his actions or lack of actions, depending on the situation. But I have found that these male figures are still men. They just haven't learned to function in the full capacity of being a man. We, as men, learn from all the wrong sources of what being a man consists of. These views are often distorted and built from men who have been hurt and scorned. In turn, it has produced generations of men who never learn or witness the truth of what it is like to function in the compacity of being a man. My program and its concepts build upon the man and teach him that not everything he believes to be true is wrong. In fact, most if not all is true, just not the way he goes about living what he believes. Therefore, I try to live life as a living example or experience of what it is like to function as a man, so they don't have to walk the same path I walked.

I took part in this book, hoping to inspire changes in how the youth process their decision-making. Our choices in life determine the opportunities that may or may not come tomorrow. I am praying that we learn to make better choices and decisions by being more aware of the options before us.

✝ *Reality: We All Have a Choice; Choose Wisely* ✝

My name is James Hicks. I was incarcerated in the Federal Prison system for 23 years. How I got to be incarcerated in a Federal Prison for the crimes I committed still eludes me to this very day. Then, the amount of time I was sentenced never ceases to amaze me. In 1997, I committed a string of armed robberies in Tulsa, Oklahoma, over three weeks. It was the Saturday after Thanksgiving that I was apprehended and charged. By May of 1998, I was convicted on six counts of Hobbs Act Robbery Affecting Interstate Commerce and six counts of Possession of a Firearm while in Commission of a Crime of Violence. I will explain in brief detail about the Hobbs Act Robbery. This is a statute the federal government uses to enhance people's sentences charged with robbery in the state system. Basically, this statute was created for those involved in racketeering crimes, like the John Gotti's and other mob-like organizations. The crime that an individual is being accused of is more than just performing a robbery. It is saying that the individual committed a robbery that somehow "obstructed, delayed or affected the movement of commerce on an interstate level.

The actual statute is located in United States Code, Section 18, clause 1951. It reads: "Whoever in any way or degree obstructs, delays, or affects commerce (interstate commerce) or the movement of any article and or commodity in commerce (interstate commerce), by robbery or extortion or attempts or conspires so to do, or commits or threatens physical violence to any person or property in furtherance of a plan or purpose to do anything in violation of this section shall be fined under this title or imprisoned not more than twenty years, or both."

Interstate commerce means the flow of commerce originating in one state and ending in another state. For example, let's say a product is produced or manufactured in Maine. Whatever this product is, it's then shipped from Maine to Utah. The product traveled from one state through other states to reach its destination in another state. Please understand, commerce is defined as the flow of goods and services. So, in essence, the accused is said to have somehow stopped the flow of commerce (or goods and services) across state lines.

Just for the record, I committed those robberies in Tulsa, Oklahoma, on the south side. Every one of those robberies was committed in the same area of Tulsa. I never left the city or state of Oklahoma. I robbed retail businesses, and they were the last point of commerce. There can't be more interstate commerce after this. The government's threshold to prove in a trial is a bad joke. They don't even have to prove that the accused has interrupted the flow of interstate commerce. They only have to prove that the accused "could have" affected interstate commerce. There are many problems with the way this statute is used. We don't have time to cover it all. I just want you to understand my charges.

In retrospect, it's no one's fault but my own because I should have never been in prison. I am one of three siblings and an only son. My two sisters have fared well in life. I graduated from high school in June of 1991 and entered the U.S. Army in November of that same year. I enjoyed the time I spent in the military: 4 years and eight months. I had the opportunity to travel to Kansas, Germany, and Oklahoma and met all types of exciting people.

Later that same year, I was sentenced to 1,350 months. So that you don't have to do the calculations, that's 112 ½ years. Yeah, you are reading that right. I was sentenced to 112 ½ years for robberies where no one was killed or hurt seriously. In retrospect, it's no one's fault but my own because I should have never been in prison. I am one of three siblings and an only son. My two sisters have fared well in life. I graduated from high school in June of 1991 and entered the U.S. Army in November of that same year. I enjoyed the time I spent in the military: 4 years and eight months. I had the opportunity to travel to Kansas, Germany, and Oklahoma and met all types of exciting people.

I left the military with a General Under Honorable Conditions discharge. I stayed in some type of small trouble that kept costing me loss of rank, loss in pay, and time doing extra duty. I can look back and see the trouble I got into was because of my mouth. I could not keep my mouth shut when someone upset me or if I felt I had been done wrong. This was an issue that was corrected as I got older and matured. I also left the Army with a marriage that was in shambles. I wed at the tender age of 19. She was 18. We had a wonderful daughter who we both cherished. We just couldn't get it right together. It was one of those situations where you both love each other but needed time to grow up before we ventured into marriage. I must say that I was the more immature of the two. Also, neither of us could manage our finances, which was the source of much contention for us. I wasn't even a year out of the Army; we were divorced with another baby (a son) on the way. I have to admit, in my arrogance, I never saw that one coming. I don't believe in divorce, so it shook me to my core. I was dejected and went into a state of rage and self-destruction. I did so much right but couldn't get my marriage together, and it cost me, and with no family, I began to take risks that I would not have taken had I still been married. Crime.

I enrolled in college while in the Army; Kansas State University, where I met my ex-wife. I joined a worldwide fraternity, and I was happy to be a

43

part of it. Afterward, although life wasn't moving the way I wanted it to, I was making positive changes by enrolling in Tulsa Community College (now Tulsa University). I initiated plans to return to the Army and made wiser decisions about my life before the divorce. However, things slowly changed because of bad choices and decisions about who I began to hang out with. Nothing in life just happens. We shape our destiny by what we choose to do and the people we associate with. By associating with others who committed crimes, I also found myself committing crimes.

It started with my decision to smoke marijuana. I went from buying it for consumption to also selling it. It wasn't long after this that I began to sell crack cocaine and still yet before I began committing armed robberies. Each foolish decision became worse in the sense of how reckless I became. I came to a point where I just didn't value life, mine, or anyone else's. I felt as if everything and everyone I cared about had abandoned me, but this mindset didn't just start here.

As a teenager, I struggled with finding acceptance. First, with myself and then with others. My self-esteem was low. I was self-conscious about my skin complexion. I heard my entire life that I was too black, which became synonymous with being considered ugly to me. I desired to be accepted for who I was instead of how others saw me. I didn't have a clue as to who I was, and that was the problem.

Violence became a tool to let off the frustration I experienced as a teenager. I never felt I was as violent as others in my age group until I got older. Later in life, I realized I was the type of guy who let things build up in me until I exploded. At this point, some unexpected person became a victim of my rage that wasn't justified. The level of violence was never conducive to the perceived transgression. By the time my tolerance level was depleted, I had taken everything out on that person. Moreover, I carried this baggage into adulthood. I was always trying to prove to others that I could or would be more violent than the next person in hopes of being accepted. What it did was cause me to be more alienated, which in turn caused me to be more angry and bitter at life and the people who came into my life.

As I look back at the time of my incarceration, I still can't believe I lost 23 years of my life because I couldn't process reality correctly. My paradigm of life was unrealistic. I entered prison scared and determined I'd conquer that fear no matter what I had to do. I resolved to be the same destructive man I learned to be earlier in life. If violence and force were the languages of prison, I considered myself to be well acquainted with it. I used whatever amount of force necessary to survive this period of my life. That was my philosophy anyway. In truth, I was scared out of my mind and didn't want it to show.

I learned quickly that prison is not a place for people who are considered weak-minded nor a place for everyone, and I'm amazed I made it for so long in prison. My concepts on life changed dramatically by the time I was released. I went into prison still trying to fit in but came home accepting myself and who I really am and enjoying it. The thing that strikes me most about prison is the emotional pain and turmoil that men of all races, ages, and cultures are experiencing. People always talk about the level of violence inside. That is most definitely true, but the level of psychological and mental violence is worse. Being alienated from society has ill effects for everyone: inmates and staff. My experience was no different. No one prepared me for the pain of not watching my children grow up. There were nights spent awake, knowing I had destroyed my life. You learn quickly to forget about life on the outside so you can concentrate on doing your time on the inside. Nothing in your life remains the same. I was able to adjust relatively easily. I credit this to my time spent in the Army. However, everyone isn't able to make those adjustments.

I was fortunate my counselor took an interest in me. She was one of the few employees that truly did her job. She placed me in a program called "Positive Mental Attitude." The older men I met in this program were able to grasp my attention. I learned from these men and the wisdom they shared with me. This early intervention dictated how the rest of my time in prison would be done. I took programs to help me improve my thinking pattern and process. It was a slow process, but I began to evolve in my perception of the world. Two of the most impressionable courses were the "CODE Program" and the "Life Connection Program." (I was about 90 days shy of graduating from this program when I got in a fight and wasn't able to complete it. The knowledge stayed with me, however.)

Being in prison allows you to read all types of books that you would never have read due to time constraints in the world or just a lack of interest in reading. I am an avid reader, so reading was just a way of passing the time during lockdowns and other times when I didn't feel I wanted to be around others. One of the first books I read was "The Long Walk to Freedom." This is a book about Nelson Mandela. I remember reading this book and thinking if he could get out of prison and become president of his country, why couldn't I get out and do something as powerful in my country? I can't say I went through any of Nelson Mandela's atrocities. However, his experiences helped me get through the things I had to endure. Books were a good escape from the reality of being incarcerated.

I want to back up and speak about the crimes and why I was imprisoned. I began doing robberies on November 6, 1997. I committed this act because my roommate wanted me to rob the business he worked for. Initially, I refused. One evening I decided to scare him because I thought he was bluffing. He wasn't. So, over the next three weeks, I committed robberies and eventually went to prison because of it. I remember well the voice of God admonishing me that He would not allow me to get away with committing those crimes. I had a good job and did not need the money from my crimes. I did these robberies because of the adrenaline rush I'd get while doing them. On the way to perform the last one, I heard His voice tell me that I needed to stop.

After my arrest, I was sitting in the holding cell waiting to dress out to go to county jail. I heard this same voice again. It wasn't an audible sound. It was something I registered deep in my soul. It said I was indeed going to prison, but I would get out. That was it. There wasn't any flash of light or something else dramatic to happen. Just that. It was this promise that kept me sane throughout all of those years in prison. Every year I expected to come home. What I did was wrong, but what the system did was atrocious. The judgment was not consistent with what was done. He had to make this promise to me. Why? Because it was what kept me from going insane from day to day. I was still this man who didn't deal with pressure all that well whenever I first went into prison.

Well, waking up every day to 112 ½ years hanging over your head is surely considered pressure in an extreme way. This is done without dealing with the guards, administrative staff, and other inmates. I heard a man tell me one time that no man's struggle is more important than the next man's. One man may only be sentenced to 18 months and be entirely stressed to the point where he contemplates suicide. His struggle is just as difficult as the man facing life in prison or a term of a sentence such as the one I had. The pressure level may seem the same when applied, but it will not seem that way to the one it is being applied to. I learned to control my temper. There were two reasons I had to learn it: one, I was tired of paying the consequence of unhealthy choices due to it. Two, I began to realize some people around me had tempers a whole lot worse than mine. I don't care what anyone tells you; no one wants to be in a situation where someone may lose their life. So "I" began taking self-inventory. It was all a part of the process; I guess of God cleaning me up. I don't know. But I do know I love the man that I am today.

Another tool that helped me learn to think was playing chess. I learned to play chess when I was about nine years old. I was a pretty good chess player. Going to prison showed me I was just moving the pieces around. I never knew there were openings with names and variations to them. I studied many of these openings, and my chess game increased dramatically. I was never the best chess player on any yard I was on, but I was really good.

I learned the way we live life is generally the way we play chess. I lived life intuitively and impulsively. So, it's how I played chess. In chess, there is a concept known as touch and move. If you touch a particular chess piece, you have to move it. No matter your intent or the consequence of moving it, you must move it. Being the impulsive guy that I was, I touched many pieces without thinking about what I was about to do. Eventually, I learned to be careful and see the traps that were being set for my downfall. The same was true in life for me. I began seeing the traps others were setting for me and how easy I was making it for them. Nothing we do should be done without using careful thought and consideration. One of the thoughts planted in my thinking early in my incarceration was that I needed to stay out of trouble. When the laws changed, the judge would not have any reason to deny my opportunity to be released from prison. Prison was the most dangerous chess match I have ever had. The consequences were immense. I was blessed to get a draw.

What do I mean by a "draw"? In chess, there are three ways that the game can end. The first way is that one of the opponents has been checkmated. This simply means that they have lost the game. The second way is that of a stalemate. This means one of the opponents has been placed where they cannot move on their turn, and the king has not been put in check. In this case, no one wins. The last way is when both opponents agree that neither can win the game because no one has the advantage in that particular game. Some draws are forced by making the same move three or more times by both opponents. The number of times repetitive moves are made in proclaiming a draw is generally decided before the game is played. But a draw can be determined by the pieces that remain on the board that will not allow the king to be mated.

In my life, prison ended in a draw; nobody won. I didn't win, the prison system didn't, nor the government. I came out of prison sound: mentally, physically, and spiritually. However, I didn't come out whole either. I can never forget the atrocities committed against me by the system. The officers' attitudes toward inmates are demeaning at best. We were looked upon as some kind of disease or virus. This is coupled with the disturbing events you witness in prison by your fellow convicts and inmates. Even though I've never been harmed in prison physically by anyone, I have witnessed others harmed in ways that make me cringe even now, to think about it. I spent 23 years in a very violent existence where the authorities expected me to not be violent or continue to have a criminal way of thinking.

In those 23 years, I lost communication with my three children. Even though I have reached out to them, they are not wanting me to be a part of their lives. I lost so much in those 23 years, and I gained many things in that time. At 47, I made it out right before Mother's Day and my 48th birthday, June 30. I definitely didn't win, but I didn't lose either. As long as there is air in my lungs, there is a chance to win in the future. A draw in chess allows you to set the board up again and win the next game. In a way, a draw is a reset button. Life has been reset for me, and I am thankful for this reset opportunity. And this is why I say I was granted a draw.

I have been home for about two months. Things have been wonderful. By wonderful, I don't mean that I don't have any problems. The problems I have are the problems I prayed about having instead of incarceration problems. For instance, car problems, traffic aggravations, bills, marital issues, and such. These are issues normal people have. I enjoy dealing with them. I hear my co-workers complain all the time about working for $15.50 an hour or having to come to work at all. I have been told I shouldn't let people know I've been in prison for the last 23 years. However, I do because I want people to know what the federal government is doing to people of color and how fortunate they really are, most importantly. I share with people that I worked for 23 cents an hour (.23) and considered myself blessed just two months ago. I was making $180 a month and happy about it. I work about forty hours or more every week and bring in about $2000 a month. So, I don't complain. I work, go to church, and stay at home. This is my routine, and I love it.

It's not about trying not to go back to prison for me. For me, it's about enjoying my freedom now. I have prepared for this my entire time in prison. I pay attention to the simple things in life. I can get in my car and drive anywhere I want at any time I want. That's a wonderful feeling. I'm able to step outside of my home in the middle of the night. That is awesome to me. I can cook on a stove, grill in the backyard, eat ice cream whenever I want, and other small luxuries that returned to me.

Since my return to society, I have spent Mother's Day with my mother for the first time in years. I'm married to a beautiful woman, employed with Amazon, acquired my driver's license, and currently doing the leg work to open my own business. These are things I've dreamed about for so long. Now, I have the opportunity to chase my dreams. I am going to run until I have fulfilled them.

I constantly think about the good men I left behind. I'm currently building a platform to advance the topic of men sentenced to too much time for crimes they committed. I can never forget the atrocity committed to sentencing me to 112 ½ years. There are still too many incarcerated with sentences similar to mine or worse. Some people are first-time offenders, the same as I. The federal government's sentences say that we are not worthy of a second chance. They are, in essence, saying these men, such as myself, cannot be redeemed. Yet, we claim to be a Christian country. Other people are just as deserving as I was in being granted a second chance of having freedom restored. Since I've been home, my mindset has been the same as when I was in prison for those last ten years or so. I accept the responsibility that comes along with freedom. I accept the joys of life as well as the hardships. I no longer possess temper or anger issues. I can laugh in the face of adversity now because the only adversity greater than the one I have come from under is death.

Life is beautiful and meant to be lived that way. I refuse to be bitter or blame others for my past decisions that caused me to be incarcerated. I don't blame the snitches or anything else. Those were my decisions and choices. I can explain "why" I made those choices, but I can never place the blame on anyone else. If I had not committed those crimes, no one could have told me that I did. Other people have gone through a divorce and other misfortunes in life without turning to crime. So, in the end, there was no excuse. If I'm going to be upset with anyone for that time lost, it has to be myself.

Was that time really lost? No, it wasn't. Like the Nelson Mandela story, mine will have a powerful ending. I will be a blessing to the communities where I reside. I will be a beacon of light for whoever wants to come from under the life of crime. I will be that example to others, letting them know they can come from a disastrous past and be redeemed. I live life in the moment now. I enjoy each moment for what it is— a moment. Nothing lasts forever in this life. So, I take comfort during the storms of life that this too shall pass. My attitude is upbeat, and I don't expect everything in life to go my way. I'm just living life one spectacular moment at a time. I do get down for moments. That's just a part of life, but the part doesn't define the whole.

There are times when I just stop and smile or laugh out loud. I think in my mind, "Man, I'm really out of prison after all those years." Have you ever prayed and hoped for something for so long that you are amazed for a long time after that when it comes? Well, that's me. Some days I'm amazed all day long. Other days, life is moving so fast I can't seem to keep up. I'm still learning all the functions of my phone and how to get around Memphis, where I live. It's funny because I didn't even recognize the small city I'm from when I was there for a few weeks. I want to leave everyone with the courses I took in prison that positively affected me. It helped me adjust to life outside by providing parenting classes, computer classes, behavior modification courses, and educational classes that contributed to joining society again as a productive citizen.

Susanne Bunton

Susanne Bunton, a Savannah, Georgia native, has also lived in South Korea, Hawaii, Connecticut, and North Carolina. She has two beautiful children, Faith, age 12, and Elijah, age 11. Susanne studied Psychology at Mid-America Christian University, where she obtained a Bachelor of Science. She's served Jesus for thirteen years. She recently obtained a license in ministry through the Pentecostal Church of God. Her heart is aimed at helping others overcome the trials and struggles of life that she has overcome herself due to the merciful hand of God that pulled her out. Susanne dreams of opening and naming her ministry Inside Out Ministries as her full understanding of God's radical transformation from the inside out.

☩ *I Stand Corrected* ☩

Two-thousand one hundred seventy-two is the number of times I was counted. Counted means you must stand up, no matter what time it is, and stand still along a very cold, white concrete wall while guards march up and down the corridor, counting every inmate until everyone is accounted for. My inmate ID number was 17164-021. My bed number was 912, and my cube (cell) number was 112. The number of days I served was 543. I was charged with 22 counts and pleaded guilty to the 11th. We are minimalized to a number more times than we realize in our lives. We were separated by birth dates, social security numbers, income brackets, age, and more. We were often seen as only a number among the rest while labeled inmate, patient, student, citizen, and for some, soldier. It's one thing to be seen as a number, but an entirely different perspective to be seen as nothing but that number.

We are…

• human beings
• have purpose
• have value
• will do great things, even if those great things are only seen by a few

We have desensitized ourselves to the point that the thought we can be replaced takes over the importance of our existence. We reject people and throw them out like trash. When the government wants you, they will get you. No one is immune. It can happen to you, your mama, daddy, children, grandma, and granddaddy. I served time beside all such people. You are about to read my journey of imprisonment. My name is Susanne. I am currently forty-three years old and went into the federal prison system at age 35. My daughter, Faith, was about to turn three years old and my son, Elijah, was about to turn two years old. Like many behind bars, our stories of being held captive begin long before entering prison doors. My hope is that my words and my story will touch someone. Even if it's just one, in such a way that you become free, and that newfound freedom you obtain becomes the new path that takes you around the struggles I survived.

On March 24, 2008, I married a man I had known for two weeks. It's obvious I did not know him, but he spoke about a Jesus I had never known and desperately wanted hope. We were both addicts at the time, and our preference was crack-cocaine. As a crackhead, my only desire was to get more crack, and it didn't matter how I got more. One night, my new husband realized what happened to me when I had been up for one too many days and hadn't eaten in several. I would have seizures. I smoked so much crack that it replaced my need for sleep or food, and the cycle continued until my brain seized up entirely. The only true sign that proved this occurrence in my eyes was that my fingernails carved indentions in the palms of my hands. I never believed people when they told me I had just had a seizure. I'm not sure if that was more because I didn't remember having it or because I just wanted more crack and knew nobody would give it to me if they knew I just died for a few minutes. Still, the seizures didn't stop my husband from bringing me more crack. It wasn't until we smoked crack with a pastor that we woke up from our destructive tendencies.

We decided to leave the state of Georgia. We had less than seventy dollars to our name but left state lines by faith that God would care for us. And God did come through, many times. We just didn't know when to stick with our blessings and cut out the curses. God had worked miracles in our lives. We drove to North Carolina and stopped at a town called

Marion. Marion was also my grandmother's name, who was on her death bed when we found the town. We stayed in a tent for maybe ten days until God opened a door that provided us with a beautiful home with a bristling creek behind it. It was breathtaking. However, this wasn't enough to prove God's love to us. I was willing to grow closer to Jesus and become free, but my husband was not.

One night, we had no money, and my husband (we'll call him DJ) wanted to get high. DJ was working at a truck stop restaurant and had been given a bag of meth. Meth was one drug I had never experienced, and it didn't take me long to figure out that I didn't like it. When the meth ran out, we found our preferred drug of crack cocaine. DJ was ready for more and, without money, the only way to get more was to sell something. I was all he had to sell. He ordered me to go "meet" some guys while getting his rock and driving around the corner. I ran off before anyone could touch me as I didn't know he planned on leaving me there. When we got back to our beautiful, God-given home, he proceeded to severely beat me. I was hit harder than I had ever been hit before. He beat me like he would beat a man. The awesome part is that the police had come to our house for an entirely different matter within hours. DJ went to jail. However, a normal person would have run back home to their mama. I sat around and waited for him to get out. I felt guilty for obeying his commands to trade sexual acts for drugs as if I were the one who wanted to do it. I believed the lie that Satan wanted me to believe. I believed the negative thoughts and voices that told me I would have traded myself if he didn't order me to do so. But, deep down, I knew I wouldn't have looked for the drugs to begin with. Yet, I still fell victim to Satan's plot, his dangerous web of deceit. My self-esteem was so low that I felt it was my duty to make it up to him. That's how addicts think. We hate ourselves for doing drugs, then we hate ourselves more for the things we do to get drugs, and then we do more drugs to forget what we've done. It's a vicious cycle.

DJ was a runner. He had been running all his life. He was running from God, from family, from normalcy, from anything that he could suspect wasn't valid. Mainly, he ran from himself. He was also running from the authorities. Because of the charges he received the night he beat me up, he was placed on probation. DJ couldn't handle facing consequences, so he forced us to move from our beautiful God-given home to be homeless, once again. We had a small painting and pressure washing business; therefore, we had the opportunity to set up shop wherever we traveled. DJ was very good at sales, so knocking on doors to pressure wash dirty homes came naturally. He always prayed to God for the work, for God to show him which door to knock and what price to give. God always provided. Many would say no, but we never went to work and came home without working. NEVER!

So, we worked our way out of North Carolina and into the mountains of North Georgia, in a town called Clayton. It was also a beautiful town. I was very glad to be back in Georgia, although I was still eight hours away from family. My grandmother had already passed by this time, as did DJ's father. My grandmother was the epitome of love. She never met someone she didn't like. I will never forget her beaming glow of joy when she saw my face. DJ's dad was also a runner from God. In fact, we tried living with him before we originally left the state of Georgia. We were clean for two weeks, but his dad was also an addict. He fed us crack cocaine for weeks on end. At his house, DJ witnessed me having my first seizure while we were together. Due to the many characteristics between myself and my family and DJ and his, we pass down whatever negative behaviors we don't conquer to the next generation. The crazy thing is that even before I had a real encounter with God and Jesus, I had this belief it was up to me to break the cycle. I was twelve years old when I started thinking like this. I knew it was my duty to not pass down the anger, hatred, emotional instability, and frustration that I grew up with. I just thought that the only way I could do so was to not have children. That was my natural fix to a supernatural issue. We all go through it. Our mind creates strategies to deal with or solve the obstacles we face in life. This is called our carnal mindset. It's what the disciples did when Jesus was crucified, and they went back to fishing. They returned to their way rather than sticking to God's way. We are asleep before we are free from relying on our own ways, thoughts, and strategies. We are like zombies or robots, just going through the motions or doing what we think we are supposed to do because everyone else is doing it or because someone taught us to work, work, work! However, just as DJ and his dad kept running from God, it never got us anywhere. In fact, we end up worse doing things our way than we would've ended up if we had just done nothing at all. We try to fill this empty space in our hearts, minds and lives with anything we can grab, even if it doesn't fit. I tried to escape reality by resorting to the quick fix of drugs and alcohol and even sex. I replaced true love with sex. I thought someone wanting to have sex with me meant I was being loved at that moment, but love doesn't go away like the men always did afterward. Love never fails. Love never goes away. I was just too asleep to know the difference. Little did I know that this marriage was the beginning of my tremendous wake-up call.

We were in Clayton, Georgia, and had been blessed with another home. On November 22, I said a short prayer out loud, so my husband heard it. I asked God for a sign should I stay with my husband. Within five seconds, our phone rang, and it was the neighbor asking us to come over. We went immediately. She handed me a ring, after saying she had noticed that I didn't have one. This ring was beautiful. It had seven diamonds in the middle, which is God's number. And it had eleven small stones on each side of the seven, making 22 total. The ring was given to me on 11-

22. I took this as a clear sign from God that I was supposed to stay with DJ.

On my 31st birthday, three months after the big "beat down," I found out I was pregnant in January. DJ had four sons before we even met. He was convinced he couldn't have a daughter. However, because of my new faith in Jesus Christ, I spoke boldly I would have his daughter. I had no clue what I was doing, but I spoke it anyway. I didn't even know if I could have children. In fact, when I was 23, I chose to have an abortion. This abortion caused me far more grief in life rather than accepting the baby as the beautiful blessing it would have been.

After the abortion, I increased my alcohol usage and experimented with drugs I hadn't previously taken. After about a hundred relationships later, I met DJ. Then ten months later, I found that God allowed me to be a mother again. This time, there was no doubt I didn't deserve this gracious gift from God. After the pain of my first pregnancy, I wasn't turning this one down. A few weeks after this wonderful news, the cops were back at my door. I had no idea DJ was sneaking out while I was asleep and going to another woman's house and, apparently, stalking her. This time, he wasn't going to get out of jail so easily, and I had to care about more than just me. I left him to sit in that jail and drove eight hours straight back home to my mom's house. Living at my mother's house was bittersweet. I had a lot of unresolved emotions about being there. Remember, I was already addicted to drugs before I met DJ, so he wasn't the reason I started using. Like most addicts, we have unresolved childhood issues, and this was the case for me. There were a lot of triggers at my mom's house, and the main reason I began using was still very much present there. Although I didn't go back to drugs, I went back to DJ once he got out. I felt as if he were safer than where I was, although this was another lie I chose to believe. I wanted to be far away from my mom's house, and he was the only way to do that.

To summarize, I found out I was having his daughter, so I named her Faith. Since I spoke her into existence through my newfound faith in Jesus Christ as my Savior, it was only natural that I name her Faith. Little did I know I would get pregnant again three months after her arrival. DJ never stopped using drugs throughout my pregnancies. He would leave me places he shouldn't have and forced me to do all the work while taking the money and wasting it on drugs.

As I mentioned earlier, we ran a pressure washing company. I always joked about how cranking one up would always put my children at ease because that's all they heard while inside my womb. For two years of pregnancy and two years of diapers, I endured endless nights of verbal, emotional, and mental abuse. DJ would manipulate me to do whatever he wanted, and it worked. Why? Because of the one night that he beat me like a man. It took a long time for the nightmares to cease, and there was only one way they finally stopped.

On October 17, 2011, one day from my son's 1st birthday, there was a knock on my door, and it was the police again. This time, however, they wanted both of us. We were sent to Liberty County Jail. I thought it was funny going to a jail named Liberty. This time though, I knew we were wanted by the police, and we had children. So not only were we taken into custody, but my precious babies were too. Fortunately, my parents were notified and picked my babies up at the local Department of Family and Children's Services. DJ had been stealing money from an elderly woman. He finally admitted it to me after he had spent nearly half of this woman's savings, which was around twenty thousand dollars. He manipulated and forced me to drive him everywhere once he told me. He also made me keep the elderly woman occupied while he covered his tracks.

A few months before that infamous cop knock, we had a call from Secret Service. DJ made me meet with them and told me to tell them he was out of state. I did as he told me. I feared he would detect if I lied to him. I had to face him immediately afterward while he waited for me in the car with our children. Many people say I had the chance to rat him out then. I regretted not doing so many times. Still, when you're slap in the middle of something so sinister and manipulative, it's almost worse than being addicted to drugs. I was ruled and controlled by fear and torment. I also feared I would get in trouble for knowing a little of what he had done. So, little did I know, I sealed my fate that day. Because I did not snitch on him, the government labeled me not just as an accessory but as the mastermind behind the entire plot of DJ's criminal behavior. I served eleven days in county jail. During that time, women ministers came and passed out books by Joyce Meyer. The book I received was called "Tell Them I Love Them." Ironically, I had said that to my stepmom every chance I could when I called to check on my babies. I never forgot that.

After getting out, I was able to get my mind straight. DJ wasn't allowed to bond out as he was a flight risk. We had to wait a good ten months before our trial was set to begin, so in that time, I was able to attend church and heal. I didn't have a vehicle, but God provided a dear friend of mine the resources and time to faithfully take me and my children (car seats and all) to church each time service was offered. She ended up being the one to drive me to federal court the day of arraignment. As we walked into the courthouse, a beggar on the streets played "When The Saints Go Marching In" on his saxophone. I never forgot that. On June 1, 2012, I pled guilty of the 11th charge of bank fraud. Many who have experienced being indicted by the federal government know not to take it to a jury trial. I explained to my lawyer all the details I've listed here in this story, yet nobody could help me. I was told that I could use the excuse I was forced to participate if he had held a gun to my head. The government had nothing but a forged check for $200 that I cashed against me. And I did cash that check under duress as he had been on another crack binge and forced me to cash it. Somehow, that two-hundred-dollar check put me in prison for eighteen months, on probation for five years, and ordered me to pay restitution of $48,000.

After being sentenced, I was allowed one month before self-surrendering at FCC Coleman, a correctional camp between several high security federal male prisons in Coleman, Florida. I was ordered to self-surrender on July 2, 2012. Ironically, July 2nd is actually the real Independence Day. It was the day that the founding fathers agreed to the Declaration of Independence. They only signed it on the fourth. So, I originally went to jail in Liberty County and prison on Independence Day. Do you see where I'm going with this?

That month went by so quickly. I spent most of it preparing for my children. I had a dream of swimming with the dolphins, and DJ's sister volunteered to watch the babies while I was incarcerated. I asked her to visit, and she agreed. She lived in Tallahassee. She arrived and took us to the beach. She had a dolphin tattoo on her back, so I did swim with dolphins after all. I took that as God's direction for my kids to go to her and will forever be grateful to our Aunt Leah for sacrificing her life to take care of my children. She came to pick them up from me the night before I was due to surrender. I'll never forget how hard it rained that night. It was the absolute worst day of my life. I hope and pray no one ever experiences the feelings I felt the night I had to give my children up. I knew I couldn't tolerate it emotionally, and like the disciples, I went fishing. I had a friend give me pills to help with the anxiety of the whole thing. I almost didn't survive to tell this story because I didn't have the tolerance I used to have when I was addicted. However, God allowed me to live through the night, and waking up the next day meant getting into my mom's car to drive to Florida to self-surrender.

Walking through those doors is faintly remembered because of the pills I took the day before. I slept the entire car ride. Once inside, the guards thought I was drunk because I stumbled. Fortunately, I hadn't been drinking. I was taken to my cube, or cell, and slept for a few more hours. I remember thinking, God must be sending me to prison on an assignment, as I clearly wasn't guilty enough to serve time. Because of that thought, when I woke up, I went around asking people if they needed prayer. Little did I know I knew who my assignment was already. It took me many months to figure it out, but the assignment was me all along.

At the beginning of my stay at Coleman, I fought my presence there. I was focused on my appeal, and I tried to speak my release into existence just like I had spoken my daughter Faith into existence. It didn't work. I prayed every prayer and fasted every kind of fast and walked around "Jericho" several times. But I remained incarcerated. So, I made friends. I do not doubt one of them was my angel in human form. She sought me out and showed me how to draw and make things to send to my kids. Losing your kids is the most terrible thing ever. I would hear them crying for me at night, and there was nothing I could do to help them. I'd try calling them, but they were three and two years old, so most of the time, they hung up on me. The other times, nobody answered the phone. So, I decided to write them letters and knew better than to mail them. I knew they were too young to understand, but they could see I never forgot them one day. I began reading my Bible daily, and I would see God everywhere. Usually, this happened in the form of me seeing three birds. Two would depart and go a certain direction, and one would go another. This happened with all sorts of things, not just birds, so it caught my attention. It reminded me of my kids and me, especially since we were separated in different directions. One day, I craved chocolate chip cookies. I hadn't had any in a while, and there wasn't a way to get any. I didn't tell anyone about this craving, but I certainly had the thought. The next day, in the cafeteria, we were all given the biggest chocolate chip cookies I had ever seen! We had them every day for an entire month! All the ladies who had been there for decades would talk about how they've never given out huge, delicious cookies such as the ones they've given us! I could only laugh to myself because I knew Who brought in those cookies! And they were certainly special ordered! It was in the little things that I found God. In prison, little things like those cookies are, really, major things. I think I cried each time I got in line to get my tray as I saw each person carry their tray with their cookies on it. It's kind of funny that God would use such a thing to minister to me. It showed me God is into detail, and He cares about what we care about.

About a year into my sentence, I received some bad news. Aunt Leah wanted her life back and threatened foster care for my children. I learned this on my lunch break. I couldn't blame her, as I remember how hard it was for me. Plus, I didn't know it, but she was having marital issues. In federal prison, we are allowed to work. In the beginning, I made 25 cents an hour. Many complained about that low wage, but I was grateful. It costs exactly 25 cents to use the phone for one minute, and that phone call to the kids was priceless. I worked in a warehouse called UNICOR. We drove forklifts and assembled pallets of materials for desks that were sent all over the world to our government facilities.

After hearing that news, I decided to walk back to work early. I prayed while walking back, mainly chewing Satan out and telling him that he can't put my kids in foster care. When I made it to the warehouse, I looked up, and right there, in front of me, I saw a beautiful white dove. Immediately, I knew my kids were going to be ok. Like we received the cookies for a month, I began to see doves in different forms for the rest of my stay. I even had a lady give me what she called a "bird" as a cardboard cut-out because she knew I was into being creative with crafts. When I got handed what she was trying to explain, I noticed it wasn't just a bird; it was a dove. I began to call this Dove Love, as God surely gave me one each time He wanted to tell me He loves me. There's so much God did during this time; I could really go on and on about certain stories that just seem impossible. They are every bit as true as the words on this page. However, I want to explain why I listed all the numbers at the beginning of this story.

When I said my bed number was 912, that's the area code for where I am from, so naturally, God still made me feel at home. When I mentioned that November 22 was the day the lady gave me a ring. The number of stones correlated to 11-22. I also want to point out I was charged with 22 counts of felony acts but pled guilty to the 11th, but there's one more significance of 1122. I didn't realize this until I had all the time in the world in prison to think of everything I experienced in my life. I ended up realizing there is exactly 1 year, 1 month, 2 weeks, and 2 days in between the births of my babies. But it gets better.

November 22nd was the due date of the baby whom I aborted and never forgave myself. Now, every time I see the numbers 1122, I can only smile and know that my God has forgiven me so much that He's restored everything the devil has stolen. So, as you can see, God used the enemy to bring about His purposes in my life. It didn't have to be that way, though. I could have and should have sold out to Jesus before I suffered all those trials, but I thought people who sound like I do today were special and that I was not. I didn't know then that I am just as important to Him as anyone else. He loves me so much. He loves You so much! In fact, those that believe in Him are His reward for being obedient to the crucifixion. Can you imagine that? Jesus hung on a cross so He would get our hearts and souls for eternity? Before prison, I didn't know this, but God certainly changed my perspective. He saw value in me and gave me freedom behind prison doors. He gave me unspeakable joy when I had nothing to live for. He had to put me in His jewelry box (in my case, prison, but for some, it's the hospital or living on the streets, or hopefully, you don't have to go anywhere and will just say YES to Him right now). But He shined me up, removed the impurities, and has now built up my life so I can tell others how much He loves them. "Tell Them I Love Them," says God!

I was released from Coleman Camp on 9-25-2013. 925 is the code for silver. There's a verse in Scripture that says, "He will refine us like silver and test us like gold." God told me I'd be the only one leaving that day, and I was. And to send me off, there was a double rainbow in the sky right as I walked out the same doors that I walked through eighteen months previously. But the person that walked through them surely was not the same person walking out through them.

As I write the end of this, it is the 8th year anniversary of the beginning of my freedom. As a single mother, I run a pressure washing and painting business on my own, and the relationship with my beautiful children has been restored. Since my release, I went back to college and received my bachelor's degree in Psychology. Also, I have become a licensed minister and welcome any opportunity to give my testimony to help others not make the same mistakes that I did. My heart is for those held in addiction and abusive relationships. The only way I can live with my mistakes is to help others see what God did for me. He can and will do for others. I want my life to show others that it is possible. I am living proof that nothing is impossible with God!

This true story is dedicated to my Creator, God, Jesus Christ, and the Holy Spirit. Also, to those who served time with me, including all guards of Coleman Camp. A special shout-out to Erin Paul, whose voice I often hear telling me I would do this very thing. To Jeannette Ayala and Mr. Harris, who laughed with us right when we needed it most. Chaplain Bass-Garcia, God used you mightily! Patricia Butler, my angel, thank you. Jennifer Simmons, you already know. Alicia Fontenot, my sister in faith forever. Many aren't named, but you know how important you are to me! It is such a blessing to see y'all living life freely! I love you all. Ain't God Good?!?!

Georgette Jackson

✝ _Signed, Sealed and Delivered!_ ✝

Let the redeemed of the Lord say so
That there is no one or anything our God cannot restore
For we all have sinned and fallen short of His glory
Your redemption was signed in blood by Jesus Christ forevermore
What happened in your past, God has surely forgiven
You turned from your wicked ways, repented, and you began to seek
His face
With outstretched arms, Jesus welcomed you in from the valley of the
shadow of death
You no longer fear evil, for in the light of Jesus, you're safe in His warm
embrace
Your redemption has been approved and signed by the Father

When you accepted his loving son Jesus into your heart
You were sealed with the indwelling of the Holy Spirit until the day of
redemption
When you took that step, you were sealed and as the Bible says
If you take one step towards God, God will take one step towards you:
that's your part
So that one day, you will walk on streets paved with gold
Eating monthly fruit from the tree of life in the city built four-square, in
Revelation we're told

When Felons Cry

Your mind has been renewed and your old man crucified; you've been
delivered
Because of God's grace and mercy, a new life you have gained; you've
been delivered
The life you once lived, you no longer crave and have left behind; you've
been delivered
You now trust the Father to guide you and keep you sustained; you've
been delivered

Opollo's Encouragement

I would like to start by introducing myself. My name is Opollo Johnson, and I'd like to offer a few encouraging words honoring a request made by a woman I respect for her resilience and tenacity. We all need the space to grow; in our lives, we must take those moments to breathe, be still, and think. It is in those moments of clarity we find the inspiration to elevate us to what's next.

Whether in writing or other creative practices, whatever it is we do, often, we're physically there but mentally preoccupied as different aspects come to the forefront while others recede. This estrangement is not only tough on those who love us, but it makes the ability to articulate our thoughts and feelings more elusive. Because when are multi-faceted, evolving people, we must cope with complex and conflicting needs and wants.

Our lives are a complex balancing act, and the truth is, we must accept we can't be all things to all people. Sometimes the artist, creator, the thinker must take a backseat to the parent and nurturer. The trick to this is knowing when to pull out of ourselves, not being overwhelmed by our frustrations, and acknowledging our progress. If our goals mean anything, we do not give them up easily. We must stay grounded, physically, mentally, emotionally. Knowing at this moment, we have the power to create. Be encouraged.

Made in the USA
Coppell, TX
22 October 2025

61439158R80046